AIR FRYER
COOKBOOK

In the
KITCHEN

AIR FRYER
COOKBOOK

In the KITCHEN
ALLISON WAGGONER

NATIONAL TELEVISION HOST, CHEF, AND AUTHOR OF
IN THE KITCHEN: A COLLECTION OF HOME & FAMILY MEMORIES
AND *IN THE KITCHEN: A GATHERING OF FRIENDS*

FRONT TABLE BOOKS | AN IMPRINT OF CEDAR FORT, INC. | SPRINGVILLE, UTAH

ISBN 13: 978-1-4621-1809-0

Published by Front Table Books, an imprint of Cedar Fort, Inc.
2373 W. 700 S., Springville, UT 84663
Distributed by Cedar Fort, Inc., www.cedarfort.com

LIBRARY OF CONGRESS CATALOGING-IN-PUBLICATION DATA

Waggoner, Allison, 1966- author.
In the kitchen. Air fryer cooking / Allison Waggoner.
pages cm
Includes index.
ISBN 978-1-4621-1809-0 (hardback)
1. Roasting. 2. Hot air frying. I. Title. II. Title: Air fryer cooking.
TX690.W34 2015
641.7'1--dc23
2015026285

Cover design and page design by M. Shaun McMurdie
Cover design © 2015 Lyle Mortimer
Edited by Deborah Spencer

Printed in the United States of America

10 9 8 7 6 5 4 3 2

Printed on acid-free paper

Contents

Introduction

Welcome to the magnificent world of air frying.

Air fryers are revolutionary kitchen appliances that use superheated air to fry foods. But that is just the tip of the food you can cook in your air fryer.

We love the taste of deep fried foods but not the calories or mess. Air frying is an exceptional way to cook foods fast, easy, and in less time. It heats up quickly and circulates hot air internally to cook food and uniformly seal in all the natural juices. Air fryers allow you to fry, bake, grill, or steam food healthier, faster, and more conveniently.

This recipe book features breakfast, vegetables, sides, main dishes, and even desserts! These are just some of the food you will be able to cook in your air fryer. This book will work with every size and style of air fryer. You can also prepare them with induction air cooking. Let these recipes inspire you to cook healthy, well-balanced meals for you and your family.

Frequently Asked Questions

Air Frying

We love the taste of deep fried foods but not the calories or mess. Air frying is an exceptional way to cook foods fast, easy, and in less time. It heats up quickly and circulates hot air internally to cook food and uniformly seal in all the natural juices. Air Fryers allow you to fry, bake, grill, and steam healthier, faster, and more conveniently.

Cooking Times

Actual cooking times in your air fryer will vary depending on several factors: the make and size of your machine, the size of food you are cooking, the thickness of cuts, the cookware used, and the temperature of items going into the air fryer basket.

As you are learning how your machine works, test the food for "doneness" before removing it from the oven. You can use a thermometer if possible. You can always start with less time and gradually adjust. When adapting a convention recipe, slightly adjust your time cooking in an air fryer by cooking it for 20–30 percent less time. *

Bakeware

Always check with your specific machine's instructions before using any bakeware with your machine. But in most models, you can use metal, glass, and silicone. If you are looking for the ultimate crunchy and fried feel, you will want to cook your items in the air fry basket for the hot air to circulate all around your food.

Oil Sprays or Misters for Frying

Never pour oil into your machine for frying. This appliance is not to be used as a deep fryer. We recommend using good quality oil sprays or your own choice of oil in a mister when you need to spritz your food. You can use any oil: olive, canola, vegetable, or coconut. You can also use the spray in the bottom of the mesh cooking basket before cooking for easy cleanup.

Breading Foods

For foods that require breading, coat these items in small batches. Press the breading onto the food to ensure that it adheres. Spritz these items with your oil spray or mister. If breading becomes too dry, pieces may become airborne, causing smoke in the heating element.

Steaming

Check with your air fryer's instruction manual first before steaming. Most air fryers will steam food. Pour ½ cup water or broth into the bottom of your cooking basket.

*Consuming raw or undercooked meats, poultry, seafood, shellfish, or eggs may increase your risk of foodborne illness.

Air Fryer Cooking Guide

		Time (Minimum to Maximum)	Temperature Fahrenheit	Turn or Shake Halfway Through Cooking
Thin Frozen Fries		12–16	390	y
Thick Frozen Fries		12–20	390	y
Homemade Fries		15–25	400	y
Potato Wedges		15–25	400	y
Potato Chips		10–12	400	y
Roasted Vegetables		16–25	350	y
Cheese Sticks		8–10	400	y
Chicken Nuggets		6–10	390	y
Fish Sticks		6–10	390	y
Steak		8–12	360	y
Pork Chops		10–14	370	y
Hamburger		7–15	360	y
Chicken Wings		18–22	360	y
Drumsticks		18–22	370	y
Chicken Breast		10–15	360	y
Spareribs		18–25	410	y
Shellfish		12–15	360–400	y

Breakfast

Strawberry and Cream Cheese French Toast Roll-Ups, page 3

Strawberry and Cream Cheese French Toast Roll-Ups

8 slices bread, white sandwich

8 Tbsp. cream cheese, softened

8 strawberries, sliced thin

2 eggs

3 Tbsp. milk

⅓ cup sugar

1 tsp. ground cinnamon

Cut the crust from each slice of bread and flatten it out with a rolling pin.

Place about 1 tablespoon of cream cheese in a strip starting 1 inch from one end of the bread. Top with the sliced strawberries.

Roll the bread up tightly and repeat with the remaining pieces of bread.

In a shallow bowl whisk the eggs and milk until well combined.

In a separate shallow bowl mix the sugar with the cinnamon.

Dip each bread roll in the egg mixture, coating well, and then roll each one in the sugar mixture.

Place in an air fryer basket seam-side down. Spray lightly with canola oil spray. Cook in batches until golden brown at 330 degrees for 5 minutes.

Biscuit Beignets with Praline Sauce

Praline Sauce

8 Tbsp. butter

1 cup brown sugar

3 Tbsp. milk

3 Tbsp. vanilla extract

¼ cup chopped nuts, pecans or walnuts

Beignets

1 tube large flaky-style biscuit dough

3 Tbsp. powdered sugar

For the Praline Sauce

Melt butter in a medium, heavy-bottomed saucepan over medium heat. Add brown sugar and whisk until sugar melts and mixture begins to boil, about 5 minutes. Stir in milk, vanilla, and nuts until smooth. Set aside.

For the Beignets

Separate biscuits and cut into fourths. Spray each side with a light spray of canola oil.

Bake at 330 degrees for 10 minutes in single layer batches so that the biscuits do not touch and have room to expand. Biscuits will cook very quickly.

Dust generously with powdered sugar and serve immediately with Praline Sauce.

Biscuit Beignets with Praline Sauce, page 4

German Chocolate Donuts, page 7

German Chocolate Donuts

½ cup chocolate frosting

1 Tbsp. water

1 can large flaky-style biscuit dough

¼ cup pecans

¼ cup flaked coconut, toasted

1 cup German chocolate frosting-flavored frosting

In medium bowl, stir chocolate frosting and 1 tablespoon water until smooth. Set aside.

Separate dough into 8 biscuits; gently roll them down to ½ inch thick with a rolling pin. With a 1-inch round cutter, cut a hole in the center of each biscuit.

Meanwhile, in small bowl, mix pecans and coconut.

Spritz each side of each biscuit with canola oil spray.

In batches, place the biscuits in the basket in a single layer and not touching.

Bake at 330 degrees for 10 minutes until golden.

Lift donuts out of the basket with tongs and frost each top with German chocolate frosting. With a spoon, drizzle the previously prepared chocolate frosting over the top.

Sprinkle with pecan mixture. Serve warm or cool.

Note: This is a great basic for all things donuts—you can top them with just chocolate or add coconut or nuts. This list is endless!

Lemon Blueberry Coffee Cake

Cake

½ cup quick or old-fashioned
   rolled oats

1 cup flour

¼ cup brown sugar

1 Tbsp. baking powder

1 Tbsp. finely grated lemon peel

2 Tbsp. all-vegetable shortening

½ cup milk

2 large egg whites, lightly beaten

½ cup blueberries, fresh or frozen,
   well drained

Glaze

¼ cup powdered sugar

1-2 tsp. lemon juice

1 tsp. finely grated lemon peel

For the Cake

Lightly spray 2 mini loaf pans or 2 individual pot pie pans with a canola spray.

Place oats in a blender or food processor and process about 1 minute. It will look like a coarse flour.

Combine oats, flour, brown sugar, baking powder, and lemon peel in large bowl. Add shortening with a fork, mixing in until mixture resembles coarse crumbs.

Stir in milk and egg whites just until blended. Fold in blueberries. Spoon into prepared pans.

Bake 1 pan at a time at 300 degrees for 15 minutes. Cool slightly. (Since this makes 2, you may need to cook them in batches. Freeze one for later!)

For the Glaze

Mix powdered sugar and lemon juice in small bowl. Drizzle over coffee cake. Sprinkle with lemon peel.

Lemon Blueberry Coffee Cake, page 8

Bacon and Egg Crescent Squares

1 can refrigerated crescent roll

4 eggs

2 slices bacon, cut in half widthwise, then halved lengthwise

4 tsp. grated Parmesan cheese, divided

salt and pepper

1 Tbsp. fresh chopped basil

Open and unroll the crescents onto a clean dry surface. Split the dough right down the middle, then in half to form 4 rectangles. Pinch the perforations together in each rectangle.

Fold up the edges of each section of dough (about ½-inch edge around each rectangle). Place 1 rectangle in the air fryer basket and then crack 1 egg into the center of it. Place 2 of the bacon sections across the egg on each square. Sprinkle with 1 teaspoon of Parmesan cheese and salt and pepper to taste. Add a portion of the basil.

Bake in the oven at 300 degrees for 10 minutes, until the edges of the crescent dough are golden brown and the egg is cooked to your preference. Repeat with remaining dough sections (baking in batches as needed, not letting the squares touch in the air fryer).

Crispy Cheesy Hash Brown Casserole

½ (10.5-oz.) can cream of chicken soup

½ cup sour cream

½ tsp. salt

1½ cups shredded hash brown potatoes

⅓ cup chopped onion

1 cup shredded cheddar cheese

½ cup breadcrumbs

2 Tbsp. butter, melted

2 scallions, finely chopped (optional)

In a large bowl, whisk together soup, sour cream, and salt. Stir in hash browns, onions, and cheese until well mixed. Spoon evenly into a 6-inch square baking dish.

In a medium bowl, mix together breadcrumbs and butter. Sprinkle evenly on top of hash brown mixture.

Bake uncovered for about 15 minutes at 300 degrees, or until hot and bubbly. Allow to rest for 5 minutes before serving. Garnish with sliced scallions if desired.

Greek Feta Baked Omelet

3 eggs, lightly beaten

3 Tbsp. frozen leaf spinach, thawed and drained

2 Tbsp. crumbled feta cheese

6 cherry tomatoes, quartered

⅛ tsp. oregano

Spray a 6-inch square baking dish with nonstick spray. Pour in eggs and top with spinach, cheese, tomatoes, and sprinkle the top with oregano.

Bake at 330 degrees for 8–10 minutes.

Maple-Glazed Donuts

1 can large flaky-style biscuit dough

¼ cup butter, melted

1½ cups powdered sugar

2 tsp. maple extract

1–2 Tbsp. milk

Separate dough into 8 biscuits. With a 1-inch round cutter, cut a hole in the center of each biscuit. Dip both sides of each biscuit in melted butter; place on a cookie sheet. (You can also dip the holes in the butter and place on the cookie sheet.)

Bake in an air fryer basket in batches at 330 degrees for 10-12 minutes or until golden brown. Remove donuts (and holes) from the basket to the cooling rack. Cool about 15 minutes.

In medium bowl, place powdered sugar and maple extract. Add 1 tablespoon milk; stir until combined. If needed for dipping consistency, stir in remaining milk. Dip each donut (and hole) halfway into icing. Place on cooling rack placed over paper-lined cookie sheet.

Baked Eggs in Brioche

3 brioche rolls, (about 3 × 3 inches in size)

3 Tbsp. butter, melted

3 slices American cheese, or cheddar

salt and pepper, to taste

3 eggs

1 Tbsp. chives

Cut off tops of brioche (about 1 inch) and scoop out insides of bottoms to make a shell, leaving ¼ to ½ inch all around and being careful not to tear. The inside opening should be just big enough for 1 large egg. Brush insides and cut edges of tops with butter. Add 1 slice of cheese to the inside of each roll.

Arrange brioche shells air fryer basket and season with salt and pepper. Crack an egg into each brioche and sprinkle with chives. Bake brioche 7-9 minutes at 330 degrees.

Serve each brioche with its top for dipping in egg.

Baked Eggs in Brioche, page 12

Morning Cheese Danish, page 15

Morning Cheese Danish

1 (8-oz.) pkg. cream cheese, room temperature

⅓ cup sugar

3 eggs, room temperature, divided

2 Tbsp. ricotta cheese

1 tsp. vanilla extract

¼ tsp. salt

1 Tbsp. grated lemon zest

2 sheets prepared puff pastry, defrosted

1 Tbsp. water

cherry preserves

In an electric mixer, combine the cream cheese and sugar on a low speed. With the mixer still on a low speed, add two egg yolks, ricotta cheese, vanilla extract, salt, and lemon zest. Mix until combined. Do not over mix or whip.

On a lightly floured cutting board, unroll 1 sheet of the puff pastry. Line a cookie sheet with parchment paper. Cut the puff pastry into square pieces, approximately 6 inches, and place, separated, on the cookie sheet. Then place a tablespoon of the cheese mixture into the middle of each square.

In a small bowl, combine 1 beaten egg and 1 tablespoon water to make an egg wash. Brush the borders of each pastry with the egg wash. Fold 2 opposite corners toward the center of each pastry so they touch and stick together. Brush the top of each pastry with the egg wash. Repeat this with the second sheet of puff pastry.

Refrigerate for 20 minutes.

Bake at 330 degrees for 10-15 minutes until the pastries are lightly brown. Bake in batches as needed. When cooled, add a spoonful of cherry preserves on the top and serve!

Egg & Cheese Strata

3 slices whole wheat bread

1 large egg, lightly beaten

½ cup whole milk

½ cup grated cheddar cheese,
    divided

sea salt

black pepper

1 thin slices prosciutto

3 asparagus spears, cut into
    5-inch lengths (tops only)

1 Tbsp. chopped chives

Butter a small 4-cup ovenproof baking dish.

Remove the crusts from the bread and cut into cubes; you should have about 1½ cups. Place the cubes into the baking dish.

Whisk together the eggs and milk in a large bowl. Stir in half of the cheese and season with salt and pepper. Pour ¾ egg mixture over the bread cubes.

Cut the prosciutto into 1-inch squares and lay over the coated bread and top with asparagus spears. Pour the remaining egg mixture over the top and top with the remaining cheese.

Bake the strata at 330 degrees until just set, 15 minutes. Let cool slightly, sprinkle with the chopped chives, and serve in the baking dish.

Egg & Strata, page 17

Parmesan Baked Eggs, page 19

Parmesan Baked Eggs

3 Tbsp. butter

1 Tbsp. minced fresh rosemary

½ Tbsp. minced fresh thyme

1 shallot, minced

6 tsp. heavy cream

6 eggs

3 Tbsp. grated Parmesan cheese

salt and pepper, to taste

In 3 small ramekins, evenly divide and place the butter, rosemary, thyme, and shallot. Place the ramekins in an air fryer basket and heat at 350 degrees for 2 minutes until melted.

Remove the air basket from the fryer. Add 2 teaspoons heavy cream to each ramekin, and crack 2 eggs into each ramekin without breaking the yolks. Sprinkle the cheese over the top of each ramekin and return to the oven. Bake for 7-9 minutes at 350 degrees.

Remove from oven when the egg whites are just set and yolks are still soft. Let stand for 3-5 minutes before serving. Season with salt and pepper.

Sweet Crunchy Granola, page 21

Sweet Crunchy Granola

1 cup rolled oats, uncooked

¼ cup flaked unsweetened coconut

¼ cup sliced almonds

¼ cup chopped walnuts or pecans

3 Tbsp. vegetable oil

pinch of salt

3 Tbsp. maple syrup

1 tsp. vanilla extract

1 cup chopped mixed dried fruit (raisins, cranberries, cherries, diced pineapple, diced apricots, dates)

In a large bowl, combine the oats, coconut, and nuts. Mix well.

In a separate bowl, combine the oil, salt, maple syrup, and vanilla. Pour over the dry mixture, stirring until combined.

Place in the air fryer basket. Bake at 300 degrees for 8 minutes. Stir and bake for another 8 minutes.

When the granola is a light-to-medium golden brown, remove it from the oven and cool completely.

Transfer the granola to a large bowl, and mix in the dried fruit. If stored in a tightly closed container at room temperature, it will last for several weeks. Freeze for extended storage.

Sweet-and-Spicy Bacon

1 lb. thick-cut bacon (about 12 slices)

1½ Tbsp. brown sugar

¼ tsp. cayenne pepper

¼ tsp. black pepper

Cut the bacon in 2 or 3 equal sections to fit along the air fryer basket.

Stir together the brown sugar, cayenne, and black pepper in a bowl. Add the bacon a few slices at a time until all slices are covered in the mixture.

Arrange the bacon slices in 1 layer (not overlapping) in the basket.

Bake at 350 degrees for 6–8 minutes in batches.

Salted Caramel Flake Donut

1 can crescent dinner rolls

1 (4-oz.) can vanilla pudding

2 Tbsp. caramel ice cream topping

¼ tsp. kosher salt

½ cup powdered sugar

1–2 Tbsp. milk

Separate crescent dough into 4 rectangles. Firmly press perforations together to seal. Stack 2 rectangles on top of one another. Fold in half widthwise to make a tall stack. Repeat with remaining 2 rectangles.

To make 2 donuts, use a 3-inch biscuit cutter to cut 1 round from each stack; use a ½-inch biscuit cutter to a cut small hole in the center of each round. Reroll and reform remaining dough to cut third donut.

Place in air fryer basket in a single layer and spray each side lightly with canola oil. Bake at 330 degrees for 10 minutes. Cool 5 minutes.

Carefully split donuts in half. Place pudding in a plastic bag with the corner cut off and pipe some pudding onto the bottom half of each donut. Top each with some caramel sauce and sprinkle with salt. Cover with each donut top.

In a small bowl, mix powdered sugar and enough milk for spreading consistency. Spread on donut tops. Drizzle with additional caramel sauce.

Note: Substitute the caramel ice cream topping with the Homemade Salted Caramel Sauce on page 25 for an extra treat!

Sweet-and-Spicy Bacon, page 22

Homemade Salted Caramel Sauce, page 25

Homemade Salted Caramel Sauce
(Use with Salted Caramel Flake Donut, page 22)

1 cup sugar

¼ cup water

1 tsp. light-colored corn syrup

½ cup heavy whipping cream

1 Tbsp. vanilla extract

½ tsp. salt

Gather all your ingredients and tools in one place, including oven mitts and a glass jar or heat-safe container. You'll be working with boiling sugar and will need to watch over it carefully.

In a medium to large stainless steel saucepan (it should be much bigger than you think you'll need because the sauce will bubble very vigorously toward the end of the cooking), add the sugar, water, and corn syrup. Bring it to a boil over high heat, whisking until sugar has dissolved.

Allow the mixture to boil for 5–12 minutes, in order for it to turn caramel colored. The final stage is where the mixture turns from pale amber to that perfect shade of caramel. This stage can go quickly, in less than 30 seconds, so don't take your eyes off it! While boiling, you don't want to whisk, but you can gently stir. As soon as the sauce has turned caramel-colored, reduce the heat to low.

Very carefully and slowly, add the cream. You need to do this with caution because the mixture will bubble up. Repeat this step with the vanilla and salt.

Whisk until sauce is smooth and combined. Let it boil another minute, which helps thicken it up.

Transfer the sauce to a glass jar or heat-safe container. Allow the sauce to cool uncovered to room temperature; the sauce thickens considerably as it cools. The sauce will keep airtight at room temperature for at least 1 month.

Sausage, Egg, and Cheese Breakfast Roll-Ups

3 eggs

1 can refrigerated crescent rolls

8 breakfast sausage links, cooked

4 slices cheddar cheese

salt and pepper, to taste

In a small bowl, beat the eggs. Reserve 2 tablespoons beaten egg for brushing on the tops of the crescent rolls.

Scramble remaining eggs.

Unroll the dough onto a work surface. Separate the dough into 8 triangles. Cut the cheese slices in half. Place 1 half on each triangle. Top each with 1 spoonful of scrambled eggs and 1 sausage link. Loosely roll up the triangles as directed on the can.

Place roll-ups, in batches, in an ungreased air fryer basket.

Brush the reserved beaten egg on top of each crescent. Sprinkle salt and pepper over each.

Bake at 330 degrees for 12-15 minutes.

Note: You can double this recipe up and freeze any remaining roll-ups. They heat up beautifully from frozen in your air fryer in 4–5 minutes on those busy mornings!

Vegetables & Sides

Perfect French Fries, page 29

Perfect French Fries

1 large russet potato, cut into
¼-inch slices

1 Tbsp. canola oil

½ tsp. sea salt

Rinse the cut potato under running water. Place the potato slices in a single layer on a microwave-safe plate. Microwave for 3 minutes. Remove from microwave.

In a large bowl, toss the slices with oil and salt.

Place the fries evenly in the air fryer basket. Do not overcrowd.

Bake at 400 degrees in a single layer for 10 minutes. Remove the basket and toss.

Return to the oven for another 5 minutes at 400 degrees.

Enjoy!

Homemade Ketchup

1 (28-oz) can whole tomatoes in
purée

1 medium onion, chopped

2 Tbsp. olive oil

1 Tbsp. tomato paste

⅔ cup dark brown sugar

½ cup cider vinegar

½ tsp. salt

Purée the tomatoes in a blender until smooth.

Cook the onion in oil in a 4-quart heavy saucepan over moderate heat, stirring, until softened, 6–10 minutes. Add the puréed tomatoes, tomato paste, brown sugar, vinegar, and salt. Simmer, uncovered, stirring occasionally, until very thick, about 1 hour.

Let cool slightly. Purée the ketchup in 2 batches in blender until smooth. Chill, covered, at least 2 hours.

Ketchup can be chilled up to 3 weeks.

Air-Dried Herbs

Take any herbs you would like. Wash and set them in an air fryer basket.

You may want to put your rack on top of the herbs as they dry. Be patient, because this will give you great results as you fine-tune the time on your machine.

Bake at 170 degrees for 20 minutes. You will need to watch over these carefully. Depending on the size and cut of herbs, you may need to go more or less time. Set them on a baking sheet overnight to cool. Then store them in an airtight container.

Avocado and Feta Egg Rolls

Egg Rolls

24 egg roll wrappers

2 ripe avocados, cut into ¼-inch pieces

4 Tbsp. chopped sun-dried tomatoes

¼ cup feta cheese

½ Tbsp. finely chopped garlic

salt and pepper, to taste

Sauce

1 avocado

¼ cup buttermilk

2 Tbsp. Greek yogurt

2 Tbsp. freshly squeezed lime juice

1 Tbsp. chopped fresh cilantro

1 tsp. minced garlic

For the Egg Rolls

In a large mixing bowl, lightly stir together the chopped avocado, sun-dried tomatoes, feta, garlic, salt, and pepper.

Working with 1 wrapper at a time, place 1 tablespoon of filling in the wrap. Brush the edges with water and roll like a burrito. Seal with more water. Repeat until all rolls are complete.

Lightly spray with canola oil on all sides.

Bake for 10–12 minutes at 400 degrees in a single layer, turning once during cooking.

For the Sauce

Place all ingredients into a food processor and process until smooth.

Bloomin' Onion Straws

1 large sweet onion, sliced very
 thin

large bowl of ice water

1 cup self-rising flour

1 tsp. salt

1 tsp. pepper

1 tsp. paprika

1 tsp. garlic powder

canola oil spray

Let the onions soak in the ice water for at least 10 minutes.

In a gallon-size ziplock bag, mix the flour with the salt, pepper, paprika, and garlic powder.

Using a pair of tongs, remove the onions from the ice water. Shake off excess water. Place the onions in the bag and toss in the seasoned flour.

Remove the onions from the bag and shake off all the excess flour. Place an even row of onions in the basket. Do not overcrowd. Evenly spray the onions with canola oil spray.

Bake in batches at 410 degrees for 14 minutes. After 7 minutes, turn the onions and spray again with oil.

Bloomin' Onion Sauce

1 cup mayonnaise

3 Tbsp. chili sauce

1 tsp. chili powder

⅛ tsp. cayenne pepper

Mix together and chill.

Kale Chips, page 33

Kale Chips

1 large bunch kale

canola oil spray

Wash and dry the kale. Remove the large rib in the center of each leaf. Cut each leaf into 1-inch pieces.

Spray them lightly with canola or olive oil spray. Season the kale with either salt and pepper or your favorite seasoning.

Bake at 250 degrees for 15 minutes, tossing halfway through.

Note: You can use any type of oil you want! You can even use sesame oil for a fun nutty taste.

Baked Brie with Figs, Walnuts, and Pistachios

4 Tbsp. fig preserves or jam, divided

⅓ cup sliced dried figs

⅓ cup chopped pistachio nuts

⅓ cup chopped walnuts

13 oz. brie cheese round

Place the fig jam/preserves in a microwave-safe dish. Microwave for 30 seconds to soften.

In a small bowl, combine the sliced dried figs with the nuts. Add half of the fig jam and mix.

Place the round of brie in a small, 6-inch oven-safe dish. Using a knife, coat the brie with the remainder of the jam.

Top the brie with the fig and nut mixture.

Place the brie dish in the air fryer basket. Bake at 325 degree for 10 minutes.

Serve with French bread or great crackers.

Artichoke and Spinach Dip

½ (8-oz.) pkg. cream cheese, softened

⅛ cup mayonnaise

⅛ cup grated Parmesan cheese

⅛ cup grated romano cheese

1 clove garlic, minced

¼ tsp. dried basil

¼ tsp. garlic salt

salt and pepper, to taste

½ (14-oz.) can artichoke hearts, drained and chopped

½ (10-oz.) pkg. frozen spinach, thawed, drained, and squeezed dry

⅓ cup shredded mozzarella cheese

bread bowl or pita chips

Mix together the cream cheese, mayonnaise, Parmesan, Romano, garlic, basil, garlic salt, and salt and pepper.

Gently stir in the artichoke hearts and spinach. Transfer the mixture to a 6-inch square baking dish. Sprinkle the mozzarella on top.

Bake for 15 minutes at 330 degrees, until bubbly and lightly browned on top. Serve in a bread bowl or with pita chips.

Artichoke and S[pi]nach Dip, page 34

Bacon Cheddar Muffins, page 37

Bacon Cheddar Muffins

extra-virgin olive oil

6 slices bacon

1 box corn muffin mix, plus ingredients according to package directions to make 1 batch muffins

1 tsp. paprika

3–4 Tbsp. chopped chives

⅓ cup cheddar cheese, shredded

Drizzle a little extra-virgin olive oil into a small skillet and place over medium-high heat. Add the bacon to the hot pan and crisp, 5–6 minutes. Remove from pan and drain on a paper towel. Chop and set aside.

Prepare the muffin mix to package directions. Stir in the paprika, chives, shredded cheese, and crisp bacon bits.

Fill the mini muffin pan with batter and bake at 330 degrees for about 15 minutes or until golden brown.

Bacon-Wrapped Cheese-Stuffed Dates

½ lb. pitted dates

½ lb. bacon slices, cut in half

2 oz. cheese, blue or goat

Make a pocket in each date by cutting a slice down 1 side. Place a large crumble of cheese into each date pocket and pinch the openings together.

Wrap each date with a piece of bacon and secure it with a toothpick.

Place the dates in an air fryer basket and bake for about 10 minutes at 330 degrees in a single layer.

Homemade Kettle Chips with Dill Dip

Chips

4 Idaho potatoes

canola oil spray

salt and pepper, to taste

Dill Dip

½ cup sour cream

½ cup mayonnaise

¼ cup finely chopped yellow onion

½ tsp. dried dill

Using a mandoline or food processor, slice the potatoes very thin.

Place the sliced potatoes in a large bowl with cold water to soak for 30 minutes.

Make the dip by stirring all the ingredients together. Refrigerate.

Divide the potatoes into 4 batches. Lay them out on a towel and dry. Spray each side with canola oil. Season with salt and pepper.

In batches, lay the slices out in an air fryer basket. Bake at 400 degrees for 5 minutes. Open and toss. Bake for another 5 minutes until crisp.

Bacon-Wrapped Cheese Stuffed Dates, page 38

Beer-Battered Onion Rings, page 41

Beer-Battered Onion Rings

¼ cup flour

1 Tbsp. cornstarch

½ tsp. garlic powder

¼ tsp. cayenne pepper

¼ tsp. salt

½ cup brown ale

1 cup fine yellow cornmeal

1 large sweet onion, sliced into
  ½-inch-thick rings

canola or olive oil cooking spray

Whisk the flour, cornstarch, garlic powder, cayenne, and salt in a medium bowl. Whisk in the ale until combined.

Place the cornmeal in a shallow bowl.

Separate the onion slices into rings and dip in the batter, letting the excess drip off. Then dredge in the cornmeal.

Place in the air fryer basket and coat the onion rings with cooking spray.

Bake in batches at 400 degrees for 6–8 minutes. Turn, coat the other side with cooking spray, and bake until browned and crispy, 6–8 minutes more.

Roasted Butternut Squash, page 43

Roasted Butternut Squash

1–2 lb. squash, peeled, seeded, and cubed

¼ cup brown sugar

2 Tbsp. butter, melted

¾ Tbsp. fresh grated ginger

1 tsp. chopped rosemary

In a bowl, place the squash, brown sugar, butter, ginger, and rosemary. Toss until coated.

Put the squash in the air fryer basket and bake at 330 degrees for 10 minutes. Toss the squash and bake for another 8–10 minutes at 400 degrees.

Bourbon Sweet Potatoes

3 sweet potatoes, peeled and boiled until fork tender

¼ cup fine aged Kentucky bourbon whiskey

1 egg, slightly beaten

¼ cup chopped pecans

¼ cup sugar

1 Tbsp. butter

⅛ tsp. grated cinnamon

⅛ tsp. grated nutmeg

Mix all of the ingredients with an electric mixer at a medium speed until smooth.

Pour all of the ingredients into a 6-inch baking dish. Bake, lightly covered with foil, at 330 degrees for 15 minutes.

Zucchini Fritter Cakes

1 small zucchini, grated

2 Tbsp. salt

4 green onions, minced

1 Tbsp. fresh chopped parsley

1 Tbsp. fresh chopped dill

1 egg, lightly beaten

¾ cup grated Parmesan cheese

¼ cup flour

Grate the zucchini into a colander in the sink; toss with salt and let sit 10 minutes.

Rinse the zucchini off under cold water. Press down in the colander to remove excess water. This next step is very important to get the most liquid off that you can. Place the zucchini on a paper towel and squeeze until almost dry.

Mix the zucchini with the minced green onions, parsley, dill, egg, Parmesan, and flour.

Take 1 tablespoon at a time and roll into a ball. Flatten just a bit. Spray each side with canola oil. Repeat with the remaining mixture.

Bake in a single layer at 330 degrees for 10 minutes until golden. Bake in batches as needed.

Zucchini Fritter Cakes, page 44

Cheesy Potatoes au Gratin, page 47

Cheesy Potatoes au Gratin

3 medium potatoes

¼ cup milk

¼ cup cream

1 tsp. black pepper

1 tsp. nutmeg

¼ cup shredded Gruyère cheese

Slice the potatoes wafer thin. In a bowl, mix the milk, cream, pepper, and nutmeg. Add the potatoes to the mixture and coat evenly.

Place the potato slices into a 6 inch pan and pour the rest of the cream mixture on top of the potatoes. Sprinkle the cheese evenly over the potatoes.

Place the pan in the cooking basket and cook at 330 degrees for 15 minutes until browned.

Cheddar Bacon Bites

2 cups finely shredded cheddar cheese

¾ cup mayonnaise

2–3 tsp. Dijon mustard

1 can large flaky-style biscuit dough

4 slices bacon, cooked and crumbled

In a large bowl, combine the cheese, mayonnaise, and mustard.

Split each biscuit circle into thirds. Press into the bottom and up the sides of the ungreased miniature muffin cups. Fill each with about 1 tablespoon of the cheese mixture.

Bake at 300 degrees for 9–11 minutes or until golden brown and the cheese is melted. Bake in batches as needed. Let stand for 3 minutes before removing from the pans.

Loaded Potato Skins filled with Bacon, Cheddar, and Sour Cream

3 potatoes
canola oil spray
4 oz. cheddar cheese, shredded

3 strips bacon, cooked and crumbled
½ cup sour cream
2 scallions, finely chopped

Microwave potatoes until cooked through.

Cut in half horizontally. Use a spoon to carefully scoop out the insides, reserving the scooped potatoes for another use, leaving about ¼ inch potato on the skin.

Place inside the air fryer basket and spray lightly with canola oil.

Bake at 400 degrees for 10 minutes until golden.

Sprinkle the insides with the cheddar cheese and crumbled bacon. Return to the oven. Bake for an additional 2 minutes, or until the cheese is bubbly. Remove from the oven. Use tongs to place skins on a serving plate.

Add a dollop of sour cream to each skin and sprinkle with scallions.

Loaded Potato Skins Filled with Bacon, Cheddar, and Sour Cream, page 48

Cottage Chips with Gorgonzola, page 51

Cottage Chips with Gorgonzola

4 medium potatoes
1 medium onion, thinly sliced

¼ cup crumbled Gorgonzola cheese
1 cup sour cream
salt and pepper

Using a mandoline or food processor, slice potatoes very thin.

In a large bowl, place the potatoes into cold water to soak for 30 minutes.

Make the dip by stirring all remaining ingredients together excluding the salt and pepper. Refrigerate.

Divide the potatoes into 4 batches. Lay them out on a towel and dry. Spray each side with canola oil. Season with salt and pepper.

In batches, lay the slices out in an air fryer basket. Bake at 400 degrees for 5 minutes. Open and toss. Bake for another 5 minutes until crisp.

French Roasted Butter Mushrooms

1 lb. mushrooms, any blend you
would like to use

1 Tbsp. butter

½ tsp. garlic powder

2 tsp. herbs de provence

2 Tbsp. vermouth

Gently brush off any dirt on the mushrooms. Quarter them and set aside.

Put the butter, garlic powder, and herbs de provence in small a microwave dish and warm until melted in microwave. Stir in the vermouth and toss the mushrooms with the mixture.

Place them in an air fryer basket and cook for 8 minutes at 350 degrees. Stir and cook for another 8 minutes, or until the mushrooms are cooked perfect to your taste.

Cheesy Pepperoni Dip with Pita Chips

6 oz. cream cheese, room
temperature

¼ cup sour cream

1 tsp. oregano

½ tsp. basil

⅛ tsp. red pepper flakes

1 garlic clove, chopped

½ cup pizza sauce

1 cup chopped pepperoni

½ cup chopped green pepper

½ cup shredded cheddar cheese

½ cup shredded mozzarella
cheese, divided

warmed pita chips

To prepare the dip, whisk together all the ingredients in a large bowl, reserving ¼ of the shredded mozzarella.

Evenly spread out the mixture in a shallow 6-inch ovenproof dish.

Bake for 10 minutes at 330 degrees until bubbly. Remove from the oven and sprinkle with the reserved shredded mozzarella. Bake for 3-5 minutes more. Serve hot with warmed pita chips.

French Roasted Butter Mushrooms, page 52

Garlic Parmesan Fries, page 55

Garlic Parmesan Fries

1 tsp. olive oil
1 clove garlic, crushed
canola cooking spray
3 potatoes

4 tsp. fresh grated Parmesan cheese
salt and black pepper

Combine the oil and crushed garlic in a large bowl.

Cut the potato lengthwise into wedges (8 wedges for each potato). Rinse them in cold water and pat dry. Place them in a single layer on a microwavable plate and microwave for 1:30 minutes on high.

Remove them from the microwave and place them in the bowl with garlic and oil. Toss in the grated cheese and coat evenly.

Season with salt and black pepper. Place in a single layer, in batches, in the air fryer basket. Bake at 400 degrees for about 10 minutes on each side, until golden brown.

Mozzarella Cheese Sticks

12 mozzarella string cheese sticks

2 eggs, beaten

2 cups Italian seasoned
   breadcrumbs

½ cup grated Parmesan cheese

½ cup flour

canola oil

Open each package of string cheese. Separate the cheese sticks and freeze for one hour.

Put the eggs in a medium bowl. In a separate medium bowl, mix the breadcrumbs together with the Parmesan cheese.

Place the flour in a large ziplock bag.

Add the cheese sticks to the bag with the flour and shake to coat them.

Take each cheese stick out of the bag, dip it in the eggs, and then dip it in the breadcrumb mixture.

Put the cheese sticks in a single layer in the basket. Do not overcrowd.

Bake at 400 degrees for about 8 minutes, turning over halfway through.

Serve with your favorite marinara as a dipping sauce.

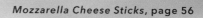

Mozzarella Cheese Sticks, page 56

Roasted Caprese Tomatoes with Basil Dressing, page 59

Roasted Caprese Tomatoes with Basil Dressing

4 large ripe tomatoes

1 Tbsp. olive oil

2 Tbsp. balsamic vinegar

1 tsp. sugar

salt and pepper

4 slices fresh mozzarella cheese, 1-2 inches thick

4 basil leaves

Dressing

20 large basil leaves

1 clove garlic

juice of ½ lemon

2 Tbsp. olive oil

salt to taste

Cut the tomatoes in half and place on a nonstick cookie sheet, cut side up.

Drizzle the olive oil and balsamic vinegar over the tomatoes, and sprinkle them with the sugar and salt and pepper.

Roast at 330 degrees for 10-18 minutes until the skins are blistered.

Remove from the oven and top each of the tomatoes with the mozzarella. Return to the oven and roast for another 5 minutes.

Remove the roasted tomatoes from the oven.

Place a large basil leaf on each of the bottom halves of the tomatoes. Top with the top half of the tomato.

To make the dressing, combine all the ingredients in a small food processor until the basil is finely chopped. Drizzle over the top of the tomatoes.

Parmesan Cream Corn

1 Tbsp. butter

2 tsp. flour

½ cup half-and-half

dash cayenne pepper

dash salt

10 oz. frozen corn

½ cup grated Parmesan cheese

Combine all ingredients in a bowl.

Place in a 6-inch square baking dish and bake for 15 minutes at 330 degrees.

Hush Hush Puppies

⅔ cup yellow cornmeal

⅓ cup flour

1 tsp. baking powder

¾ tsp. salt

⅛ tsp black pepper

½ cup finely chopped onion

⅓ cup milk

2 eggs, lightly beaten

2 Tbsp. butter, melted

Lightly grease a mini muffin pan or spray with nonstick cooking spray.

In a medium bowl, combine the cornmeal, flour, baking powder, salt, and pepper.

In a separate bowl, mix together the onion, milk, eggs, and butter. Fold the egg mixture into the flour mixture until the flour mixture is just moistened.

Spoon 1 tablespoon of the batter into each of the prepared mini muffin cups. Bake for 10 minutes at 330 degrees, or until the hush puppies are firm to the touch and golden brown around the edges. Bake in batches as needed.

Parmesan Cream Corn, page 60

Rustic Corn Bread, page 63

Rustic Corn Bread

1 cup cornmeal

¾ cup flour

1 Tbsp. sugar

1½ tsp. baking powder

½ tsp. baking soda

¼ tsp. salt

2 large eggs, lightly beaten

1½ cups buttermilk

6 Tbsp. butter, melted

Grease 2 mini loaf pans. (Or you can do them in mini muffin pans.)

In a large bowl, mix together the cornmeal, flour, sugar, baking powder, baking soda, and salt.

In a separate bowl, mix together the eggs, buttermilk, and butter. Pour the buttermilk mixture into the cornmeal mixture and fold together until there are no dry spots (the batter will still be lumpy).

Pour the batter into the prepared loaf pans, a bit over ½ full.

Bake until the top is golden brown and a toothpick inserted into the middle of the corn bread comes out clean, about 15-20 minutes at 330 degrees. Bake in batches as needed.

Torn Bread Salad with Roasted Tomatoes and Goat Cheese

8 small shallots, quartered

1½ cups grape tomatoes

2½ Tbsp. extra-virgin olive oil, divided

salt and pepper

1 cup cubed pumpernickel bread (½-inch cubes)

1 Tbsp. mayonnaise

1 Tbsp. sherry vinegar

½ tsp. Dijon mustard

2 romaine hearts, cut crosswise into ½-inch ribbons

3 oz. goat cheese, crumbled

In a medium baking dish, toss the shallots with the tomatoes and 1 tablespoon olive oil, and season with salt and pepper.

Place in an air fryer basket and bake at 370 degrees for 15 minutes, tossing halfway through. Pour into a large bowl and let cool.

Meanwhile, spread the pumpernickel cubes in the air fryer basket and toast for about 5 minutes at 330 degrees, until crisp. Let cool.

In a small bowl, whisk the remaining 1½ tablespoon olive oil with the mayonnaise, sherry vinegar, and mustard. Season with salt and pepper.

Toss the toasted pumpernickel croutons, shallots, tomatoes, and romaine with the dressing until coated.

Add the goat cheese, toss gently, and serve.

Jalapeños . . . Are Popping!

1 (8-oz.) pkg. cream cheese, softened

3 jalapeños, finely chopped

½ cup shredded cheddar cheese

coarse salt and pepper

24 refrigerated square wonton wrappers

vegetable oil spray

In a bowl, combine cream cheese, jalapeños, cheddar cheese, and salt and pepper to taste.

In a mini muffin pan, arrange the wontons in each muffin cup. Add 1 teaspoon of the filling to the center of each wonton.

Place on the fryer rack and lightly spray them with the vegetable oil.

Air fry at 350 degrees for 8–10 minutes until golden.

Parmesan Artichoke Hearts

1 (15-oz.) can artichoke hearts, packed in water

2 eggs

1 cup panko breadcrumbs

¼ cup grated Parmesan cheese

Drain the artichokes and quarter.

Mix the eggs in a medium bowl. In a separate bowl, add the panko breadcrumbs and Parmesan cheese and mix well.

Dip each artichoke in the eggs, and then coat them with the panko mixture.

Place on small plate and spray both sides lightly with canola oil.

Place in the air fryer basket in a single layer and bake at 400 degrees for 10 minutes, turning halfway through. Bake in batches as needed.

Roasted Parmesan Cauliflower

2 cups cauliflower florets

½ medium onion, sliced thinly

4 sprigs fresh thyme

4 cloves garlic, unpeeled

3 Tbsp. olive oil

salt and pepper, to taste

½ cup Parmesan cheese

Toss all the ingredients except the cheese in a large bowl.

Place in an air fryer basket and bake at 350 degrees for 25 minutes, tossing halfway through.

Once the cauliflower is cooked through, place it in a bowl and toss with the Parmesan cheese.

Greek Potatoes

½ tsp. salt

½ tsp. black pepper

½ tsp. paprika

½ tsp. dried oregano

3 garlic cloves, chopped

2 Tbsp. butter, melted

1 Tbsp. lime juice

1½ cups chicken broth

2 large baking potatoes, peeled, washed, and cut into wedges

1 cup grated Parmesan cheese

1 cup chopped parsley leaves

In a large bowl, mix the salt, pepper, paprika, oregano, garlic, butter, lime juice, and chicken broth together. After completely mixed, add the potatoes to the bowl.

Place the mixture in a baking dish. Then place the dish inside the air fryer basket. Cover with foil. Bake at 400 degrees for 20 minutes.

Uncover and sprinkle with the Parmesan cheese. Bake for another 8 minutes at 370 degrees. Sprinkle with the chopped parsley leaves.

Roasted Parmesan Cauliflower, page 66

Roasted Red Potato Salad with Mustard Vinaigrette (Cold or Hot), page 69

Roasted Red Potato Salad with Mustard Vinaigrette (Cold or Hot)

Roasted Red Potatoes

1½ lb. red potatoes, quartered

4 cloves garlic, diced

2 Tbsp. olive oil

salt and pepper

Vinaigrette

2 Tbsp. olive oil

1 Tbsp. grainy mustard

1 Tbsp. white wine vinegar

2 Tbsp. chopped parsley

salt and pepper

For the Potatoes

Add the potatoes and garlic to a bowl, drizzle with the oil, tossing to coat, and sprinkle with salt and pepper.

Place the potatoes in the air fryer basket. Roast the potatoes until crisp and golden brown on the outside and tender on the inside, about 15-20 minutes at 370, flipping halfway through.

For the Vinaigrette

While the potatoes are roasting, make the vinaigrette: Whisk together the oil, mustard, white wine vinegar, and parsley. Season with salt and pepper.

Toss the still-hot potatoes with the vinaigrette and serve warm. (Or, keep in the refrigerator and serve them cold.)

Spicy Roasted Rosemary Nuts

1 cup almonds

1 cup pecans

1 cup cashew nuts

2 Tbsp. finely chopped rosemary

2 tsp. brown sugar

1 tsp. sea salt

½ tsp. cayenne pepper

2 Tbsp. butter, melted

In an air fryer basket, combine the almonds, pecans, and cashews. Bake at 330 degrees for about 18 minutes or until toasted, stirring once.

In a small bowl, combine the rosemary, brown sugar, salt, and cayenne pepper. Stir in butter.

Once the nuts are roasted, place them in a bowl with the rosemary mixture and gently toss to coat.

Serve them warm or cooled to room temperature. Store in an airtight container for up to 7 days.

Spicy Roasted Rosemary Nuts, page 70

Sweet Potato Fries—Any Which Way!, page 73

Sweet Potato Fries—Any Which Way!

2 lb. sweet potatoes

¼ cup olive or other vegetable oil

1–2 Tbsp. sugar

1 Tbsp. salt

2 Tbsp. spice of choice

Peel the sweet potatoes and cut off the ends. Cut them in half lengthwise and then, if they are very long, in half crosswise. Cut each piece into wedges.

Rinse the potatoes with water. Place on a microwave-safe plate and microwave for 3 minutes on high.

Take the potatoes out and let them cool slightly.

Put the sweet potatoes into a large bowl and add the oil. Mix well to combine.

Sprinkle with the salt, sugar, and spices of your choice. Coat the potatoes well.

Spread the sweet potatoes out in a single layer. Bake at 400 degrees for 25 minutes, turning halfway through.

Note: Delicious and crispy—you add your own spice! Pick whatever you love! Here are a few suggestions: chipotle powder, smoked paprika, Chinese five-spice, pumpkin pie spice, garam masala, or Cajun seasoning.

Vegetable Chips

2 medium vegetables (beets, zucchini, sweet potatoes, squash, carrots, and so on)

1 tsp. extra-virgin olive oil

Peel your vegetables and slice them 1/16 inch thick with a mandoline. In a large bowl, toss sliced vegetables with extra-virgin olive oil. If you want to add a spice or salt and pepper, do so now.

In batches, lay the slices out in an air fryer basket. Bake at 400 degrees for 5 minutes. Open and toss. Bake for another 5 minutes until crisp. (You may need to cook slightly longer if you are using a vegetable with more water content.)

Stuffed Garlic Mushrooms

1 slice white bread

1 clove garlic, crushed

1 Tbsp. finely chopped flat leaf parsley

salt and pepper

1 Tbsp. olive oil

12 mushrooms

In a food processor, grind the slice of bread into fine crumbs and mix in the garlic and parsley. Salt and pepper to taste. When fully mixed, stir in the olive oil.

Cut off the mushroom stems and fill the caps with the breadcrumbs. Pat the crumbs into the caps. Place the mushrooms in the air fryer basket and slide into the fryer.

Bake at 390 degrees for 10 minutes until golden and crispy.

Vegetable Chips, page 74

Zucchini Crunch Fries, page 77

Zucchini Crunch Fries

½ cup panko crumbs

¼ cup grated Parmesan cheese

¼ tsp. basil

¼ tsp. oregano

¼ tsp. cayenne pepper

2 medium-sized zucchini

¼ cup egg whites (about 2 egg whites)

In a bowl, mix together the crumbs, cheese, and herbs. Set aside.

Wash the zucchini well; leave unpeeled. Cut in half crosswise. Then cut into wedges not more than ½ inch thick.

Put the egg whites in a shallow bowl. Put a small amount of the crumb mixture on another plate.

Dip a zucchini wedge in the egg whites to coat. Then place it in the crumbs to coat, pressing down well. Place the wedges in a single layer in an air fryer pan.

Spray the wedges lightly with canola oil. Set temperature to 350 degrees and cook for 7 minutes. Turn wedges over with tongs, and cook for another 7 minutes.

Island Coconut Shrimp, page 101

Main Dishes

Award Winning Buffalo Wings, page 81

Award-Winning Buffalo Wings

24 chicken wings

3 oz. unsalted, butter

1 clove garlic, minced

¼ cup hot sauce

½ tsp. salt

Place a 6-quart saucepan with a steamer basket and 1 inch of water in the bottom, over high heat, cover, and bring to a boil.

Place the wings into the steamer basket, cover, reduce the heat to medium, and steam for 10 minutes. Remove the wings from the basket and carefully pat dry. Lay the wings out on a cooling rack set in a half sheet pan lined with paper towels and place in the refrigerator for 1 hour.

Place in an air fryer basket and bake at 330 degrees for 30 minutes, turning halfway through.

While the chicken is roasting, melt the butter in a small bowl along with the garlic. Pour this along with the hot sauce and salt into a bowl large enough to hold all of the chicken and stir to combine.

Remove the wings from the oven and transfer to the bowl and toss with the sauce. Serve warm.

Soy Salmon Steaks

2 salmon fillets
black pepper and salt
⅛ tsp. garlic powder
lemon juice from 1 large lemon

⅓ cup light soy sauce
⅓ cup brown sugar
⅓ cup water
2 Tbsp. olive oil

Wash and pat the salmon dry with paper towels. Season the salmon fillets with black pepper, salt, and garlic powder.

In another bowl, stir together the lemon juice, soy sauce, brown sugar, water, and oil until sugar is dissolved.

Pour into a shallow dish. Place the salmon in the marinade. Cover and refrigerate for at least 2 hours.

Arrange the fish fillets on an air fryer grill basket. Bake at 330 degrees for 8 minutes or until done.

Soy Salmon Steaks, page 82

Baked Lemon Chicken, page 85

Baked Lemon Chicken

¼ cup olive oil

3 Tbsp. minced garlic

⅓ cup white wine

1 Tbsp. grated lemon zest

2 Tbsp. freshly squeezed lemon juice

1½ tsp. dried oregano

1 tsp. minced fresh thyme leaves

kosher salt and freshly ground black pepper

4 boneless chicken breasts, skin on

1 lemon

Warm the olive oil in a small saucepan over medium-low heat. Add the garlic and cook for just 1 minute, but don't allow the garlic to turn brown.

Remove from the heat, add the white wine, lemon zest, lemon juice, oregano, thyme, and 1 teaspoon salt. Pour into a baking dish.

Pat the chicken breasts dry and place them skin side up in the sauce. Brush the chicken breasts with the olive oil and sprinkle them liberally with salt and pepper. Cut the lemon in 8 wedges and tuck it among the pieces of chicken.

Bake for 30 minutes at 330 degrees, depending on the size of the chicken breasts, until the chicken is done and the skin is lightly browned. Allow to rest for 5 minutes and serve.

Crispy Asian Dumplings

24 round wonton wrappers

Filling

4 cups shredded cabbage

1 Tbsp. minced green onions

¼ cup chopped water chestnuts

1 lb. ground pork, cooked and crumbled

1 Tbsp. soy sauce

½ Tbsp. freshly grated ginger

1 tsp. sesame oil

In a large bowl, combine filling ingredients.

Place a wrapper on work surface and drop 1 heaping teaspoon of filling in the center.

Moisten edges with water using your finger tip and fold the dumpling in half and pinch to seal. Repeat with remaining dumplings.

Place the dumplings in an air fryer in batches. Spray them lightly with canola oil and bake at 400 degrees for 10 minutes, turning over halfway through.

Serve the dumplings hot with any of your favorite dipping sauces.

Crispy Asian Dumplings, page 86

Corned Beef and Swiss Cheese Melts, page 89

Corned Beef and Swiss Cheese Melts

8 oz. corned beef, coarsely chopped

1 cup shredded swiss cheese

1 (10-oz.) can cream of mushroom soup

1 Tbsp. Dijon mustard

1 tsp. caraway seeds

1 can large flaky-style biscuit dough

In a large bowl, mix the corned beef, cheese, soup, mustard, and caraway seeds until well combined.

Separate the dough into 8 biscuits. Press or roll each biscuit to form a 6-inch round for each one.

Place ⅓ cup meat mixture in center of each round.

Gently pull one side of the biscuit over and around filling, pressing the edges together to seal.

Spray the biscuits lightly with canola oil and place in a single layer, not touching, in the air fryer basket.

Bake at 330 degrees for 12 minutes.

Garlic Ginger Shrimp

2 cloves garlic, chopped

1 tsp. grated ginger

2 green onions, chopped

2 tsp. fresh squeezed lime juice

2 Tbsp. soy sauce

1½ Tbsp. sugar

3 Tbsp. butter

1 lb. shrimp, cleaned

In a small saucepan, mix all ingredients except the shrimp. Heat to simmer. Then remove from heat and let cool. This can be done a day ahead.

Place the shrimp and marinade in a bag or bowl covered in plastic wrap and marinade for at least an hour in the fridge.

Place the shrimp on a single layer in the air fryer basket. Spritz with a light coat of canola oil.

Bake at 350 degrees for 8 minutes, turning halfway through. You may need to adjust the time depending on the size of the shrimp.

Crunchy Taco Cups

1 lb. ground beef, browned and drained

1 envelope taco seasoning

1 (10-oz.) can diced tomatoes and chilies, drained

1 jalapeño, diced

24 wonton wrappers

1 cup shredded cheddar cheese

Combine the beef, seasoning mix, diced tomatoes, jalapeño in a bowl and mix well.

In a mini muffin pan, line all the muffin cups with a wonton wrapper. Spritz with canola oil. Add 1 tablespoon of beef filling to each and top with the cheese.

Bake at 370 for 8–10 minutes until hot and golden.

Garlic Ginger Shrimp, page 90

Grilled Cheese Perfection, page 93

Grilled Cheese Perfection

2 slices bread, per sandwich   butter

3 slices cheese, your choice

Butter each slice of bread on both sides.

Place one slice of buttered bread on the rack. Add the cheese slices on top of the bread. Cover the cheese with the second slice of buttered bread.

Bake at 400 degrees for 8 minutes, turning halfway through.

Note: You choose the cheese—brie, cheddar, American, swiss, provolone . . . it doesn't matter! Also, it is great to use this as a base and start adding in your own favorite toppings like onion jam, arugula, and so on.

Buffalo Chicken Bowls

2 Tbsp. wing sauce (mild or hot, according to taste)

¼ cup softened cream cheese

2 Tbsp. ranch salad dressing or blue cheese dressing

6 oz. cooked chicken breasts, diced

1½ oz. blue cheese, crumbled

12 wonton wrappers

extra blue cheese, for topping

In a large bowl, mix together the hot wing sauce, softened cream cheese, and ranch dressing. Add in the chicken and blue cheese. Stir until just combined.

In a mini muffin pan, place 1 wonton wrapper in each mini muffin cup—press down until it creates a cup.

Fill each wrapper cup ¾ of the way with the chicken mixture.

Bake for 10 minutes at 330 degrees, or until the wrappers are golden brown and the cheese is bubbling. Top with more crumbled blue cheese for garnish.

Garlic Rosemary Steak

3 sprigs rosemary, finely chopped

3 cloves garlic, finely chopped

pinch red pepper flakes

olive oil

2 steaks, 8 oz. each (can be any kind of steak)

salt and pepper

In a small bowl, combine the rosemary, garlic, red pepper flakes, and enough olive oil to make a loose paste.

Spread the mixture over both sides of each steak and sprinkle them generously with salt and pepper. Let them marinate for about 20 minutes.

Place the steaks in the air fryer basket. How long you should cook them depends on how you like your steak. Keep a close eye on these. I like to go with a thicker steak to have it more rare.

Roast at 400 degrees until your preferred doneness, about 15 minutes. Turn the steak halfway through your cooking time.

Garlic Rosemary Steak, page 94

Cheeseburger-Stuffed Baked Potatoes

Cheese Sauce

2 tsp. butter

2 tsp. flour

¼ tsp. salt

⅛ tsp. black pepper

½ cup milk

10 slices American cheese

Filling

½ lb. ground beef

¼ cup diced onion

⅛ tsp. salt

⅛ tsp. black pepper

1 tsp. Worcestershire sauce

4 Tbsp. ketchup

3 potatoes, baked and cooled

To prepare the cheese sauce, melt the butter in a small saucepan. Add the flour and cook, while stirring, for about 1 minute. Add the salt, pepper, and milk. Bring the mixture to a simmer, stirring constantly. When the sauce has thickened, remove from the heat and add the cheese. Stir until the cheese is completely melted.

To prepare the filling, brown the ground beef with the onion in a small sauté pan over medium heat. Drain off the extra fat and place the meat into a large bowl. Mix in the salt, black pepper, Worcestershire sauce, ketchup, and cheese sauce to the bowl and set aside.

Cut an opening in each baked potato, lengthwise, starting from the top of each potato.

Scoop out the flesh, creating a shell. Take ½ of the potato flesh and chop it into small pieces and set aside. (Feel free to use the other ½ of the potato flesh from this recipe in the Crispy Cheesy Hash Brown Casserole on page 10.) Repeat with each potato. Place the empty potato shells into the air fryer basket.

Mix the reserved potato flesh with the beef mixture. Fill the potato shells with the mixture.

Bake at 330 degrees for 15–18 minutes.

Pepperoni Pizza Rolls

2 Tbsp. olive oil

½ cup diced zucchini

½ cup chopped red bell pepper

4 medium mushrooms, sliced

6 oz. pepperoni, sliced

6 oz. pizza sauce

12 egg roll wrappers

8 oz. mozzarella cheese, shredded

Heat the olive oil over medium heat in a medium-size skillet. Add the zucchini, pepper, and mushrooms to the skillet and sauté until soft.

Remove the pan from the heat and let the vegetables cool slightly. Then, spoon the vegetables and 10 slices of pepperoni into a food processor with the pizza sauce.

Pulse until the vegetables are roughly chopped.

Lay out each of the egg roll wrappers. Lay 4 sliced pepperoni on each wrapper on the top ⅓ of the wrapper, leaving ¼ inch on each side of wrapper.

Place 1 tablespoon of the filling on top of the pepperoni and top with 1 tablespoon cheese. Fold the 2 sides in and then roll up in thirds. It is the same as rolling an egg roll.

Place the roll in the air fryer basket and spritz with canola oil.

Bake at 370 degrees for 8 minutes.

Lumpy Crab Cakes, page 99

Lumpy Crab Cakes

2 slices white bread

½ lb. jumbo lump crabmeat

2 Tbsp. mayonnaise

½ tsp. Worcestershire sauce

1 egg, beaten

pinch of salt

2 Tbsp. butter

Cut the crust off the slices of bread.

Tear the bread into very small pieces and add to a bowl with the crab.

Add the mayonnaise, Worcestershire sauce, egg, and salt. Mix together gently but thoroughly. Form into 4 patties.

Spray each side with canola oil. Place on a pan and then add to the fryer basket.

Bake at 370 degrees for 10 minutes, turning halfway through.

All in Chicken Nachos

2 tsp. chili powder

2 tsp. ground cumin

1 tsp. garlic powder

1 tsp. salt

2 cups chopped or shredded cooked chicken breasts

tortilla chips

2 medium tomatoes, seeded and diced

½ (15-oz.) can black beans, rinsed and drained

1 (8-oz.) pkg. shredded cheese, Mexican blend

4 scallions, chopped

¾ cup chopped fresh cilantro

1 jalapeño, chopped (optional)

Stir together the chili powder, cumin, garlic powder, and salt in a small bowl.

Add the chicken and toss evenly to coat.

Place a layer of foil in the air fryer basket to easily lift out tacos. Spread the tortilla chips in an even layer on a foil-lined air fryer basket. Evenly top the chips with the chicken, followed by the tomatoes and black beans. Finish with the cheese and scallions.

Bake for 5–10 minutes at 300 degrees. Remove from the oven and top with the cilantro and jalapeño.

Mediterranean Chicken with Dill Greek Yogurt Sauce

Dill Sauce

1 garlic clove, minced

1 cup chopped fresh dill

2¾ cups Greek yogurt

1 Tbsp. olive oil

3 Tbsp. fresh lemon juice

pinch of cayenne pepper

salt to taste

Chicken

10 cloves garlic, minced

½ tsp. paprika

½ tsp. allspice

½ tsp. ground nutmeg

5 Tbsp. olive oil, divided

8 boneless skinless chicken thighs (or breasts)

1 red onion, sliced

juice of 1 lemon

For the Dill Sauce

Combine the minced garlic, fresh dill, yogurt, olive oil, lemon juice, cayenne pepper, and salt in a food processor. Run until all the ingredients are well blended.

Transfer to a small bowl or container, cover, and refrigerate for at least 1 hour or until ready to use.

For the Chicken

In a small bowl, mix together the minced garlic, spices, and 3 tablespoons olive oil. Pat the chicken thighs dry and rub each with the garlic-spice mixture. Add the onion slices, lemon juice, and remaining olive oil. Cover and refrigerate for 1 hour or overnight.

In an air fryer basket, place the onions down in a layer on the bottom. Add the chicken thighs on top of the onions in a single layer.

Bake at 370 degrees for 20 minutes, turning halfway through. Bake in batches as needed. Serve with dill sauce.

Island Coconut Shrimp

¾ cup panko breadcrumbs

½ cup shredded unsweetened
   coconut

2 tsp. lime zest

1 tsp. salt

¼ tsp. black pepper

2 eggs

18 shrimp, peeled, deveined, and
   tails left intact

Mix the panko, coconut, lime zest, salt, and pepper in a medium shallow bowl.

Whisk the eggs in another medium bowl. Add the shrimp to the bowl with beaten eggs and toss to coat.

Working with 1 shrimp at a time, remove shrimp from beaten eggs and turn to coat each one in panko mixture.

Spritz with oil on both sides of the shrimp.

Place shrimp in air fryer basket in a single layer.

Bake the shrimp in batches at 370 degrees for 8-10 minutes, or until they are cooked through and golden. (This depends on the size of your shrimp.)

Parmesan Baked Tilapia, page 103

Parmesan Baked Tilapia

¼ cup mayonnaise

2 cups grated Parmesan cheese

⅛ tsp. cayenne pepper

4 tilapia fillets

2 tsp. lemon juice

10 ritz crackers, crushed

Mix the mayonnaise, cheese, and pepper until blended.

Place the fish in a shallow pan and drizzle with the lemon juice.

Cover the fish with the mayonnaise mixture and sprinkle it with cracker crumbs.

Bake at 330 for 10–12 minutes or until the fish flakes easily with a fork.

Wild Mushroom Pizza

4 oz. prepared pizza dough

5 oz. assorted wild mushrooms (crimini, morel, and stemmed shiitake), sliced

1½ tsp. chopped fresh rosemary

1 tsp. olive oil

salt and pepper to taste

¼ cup thinly sliced red onion

½ cup shredded Fontina cheese

Roll the pizza dough out to fit on the inside of the air fryer drawer. Place the dough inside the drawer and spray it lightly with olive oil spray. Bake at 350 degrees for 5 minutes. Turn the dough over, spray lightly with olive oil and bake for another 5 minutes until the crust is golden. Remove the crust from the oven to cool while you prepare the mushrooms.

In a 6-inch ovenproof dish, toss the mushrooms, rosemary, and olive oil. Place the dish in the air fryer at 400 degrees for 5 minutes until roasted. Season with salt and pepper.

Remove the mushrooms from the air fryer. Spread them over the pizza crust, top with the sliced onions and cheese. Return to the air fryer and bake at 400 degrees for 5 minutes until bubbly.

Note: If you love red sauce, you can add a tablespoon or 2 on top of the crust before the mushrooms.

Perfect Pork Chop with Spinach and Kale Salad

½ cup apple cider vinegar

1 Tbsp. whole grain mustard

2 Tbsp. honey

½ cup olive oil

pepper

salt

2½ cups thinly sliced kale leaves, center ribs removed

1 cup baby spinach

1 Granny Smith apple, cut into matchsticks

4 center-cut loin pork chops, each about 2 inches thick

4 tsp. fresh thyme

2 tsp. dried marjoram

For the Dressing and Salad

Mix together the vinegar, mustard, and honey in a small bowl. Gradually add in the olive oil and add a pinch of salt and pepper.

In a separate bowl, combine the kale, spinach, and apple. Add the dressing and toss to coat. Let stand for at least 5–8 minutes before serving.

For the Pork Chops

Season the meat on both sides with salt and pepper, thyme, and marjoram.

Place the pork chops in the air fryer basket. Bake at 400 degrees for 20 minutes, turning halfway through. Use an instant read thermometer to measure 145 degrees for doneness.

Mound the salad on a platter and top with the pork chops.

Perfect Pork Chop with Spinach and Kale Salad, page 104

Ravioli Cruncholi, page 107

Ravioli Cruncholi

3 eggs, whisked

2 cups flour

2 cups Italian breadcrumbs

12 premade cheese ravioli, frozen

marinara sauce, for dipping

Place the eggs, flour, and breadcrumbs in separate shallow bowls.

Working in batches, dip ravioli in the following sequence: egg, flour, egg, and breadcrumb. Coat completely.

Place the ravioli in the air fryer basket in batches (5-6 at a time, depending on size) and bake at 370 degrees for about 18 minutes, turning over halfway.

Serve with warmed marinara sauce.

Roasted Italian Sausage, Peppers, and Onions

1 lb. red potatoes, cut into large chunks

1 onion, cut into wedges

1 yellow pepper, cut into wedges

1 red bell pepper, cut lengthwise

3 sprigs rosemary

1 Tbsp. olive oil

1 lb. Italian sausage

Place all the cut vegetables and rosemary in a large bowl. Drizzle with oil and coat thoroughly.

Arrange the potatoes, onion wedges, peppers, and rosemary on the bottom of the air fryer basket. Then place the sausage on top of the vegetables.

Roast for 30–35 minutes at 370 degrees or until potatoes are fork tender and sausages are lightly browned, stirring once halfway through.

Note: The trick here is to cut everything about the same size so they cook evenly.

Roasted Italian Sausage, Peppers, and Onions, page 108

Philly Steak Rolls

1 green bell pepper, finely chopped

1 medium white onion, finely chopped

1 (6-oz.) pkg. frozen Philly-style sliced steak

½ lb. shredded provolone cheese

12 egg roll wrappers

Sauté the pepper and onion in a large pan, with a drizzle of olive oil, until they are slightly softened but still crisp, about 5–6 minutes. Set aside on a paper towel-lined plate until cooled.

In the same pan, heat the sliced meat until cooked through. Use a spatula to chop up the meat as it cooks. Cook until browned and transfer to a paper towel-lined plate until cooled.

When the meat and vegetables are cooled, add them into a large bowl with the shredded cheese. Stir to combine.

On a clean, dry surface like a cutting board, lay out your egg roll wrappers. You should only lay a few out at a time so that they do not dry out. Place ¼ cup of the meat mixture in the center of each wrapper.

Fold ⅓ of the wrapper over, fold both sides in toward the middle, and then fold over on itself. It will resemble an egg roll.

Spritz the outside with canola or olive oil spray.

Set your temperature to 350 degrees and bake for 10 minutes. Then set it to 400 degrees for another 2 minutes.

Rosemary Pork Chops & Potatoes

4 Tbsp. vegetable oil, divided

2 Tbsp. chopped fresh rosemary

1 tsp. dried oregano

1 tsp. dried basil

1½ tsp. salt, divided

¾ tsp. ground black pepper, divided

zest of ½ orange

12 small red bliss potatoes, washed and quartered into wedges

1 Tbsp. chopped garlic

4 boneless pork chops, cut 1 inch thick

To prepare the rub for the pork, combine 1 tablespoon oil, rosemary, oregano, basil, 1 teaspoon salt, ½ teaspoon black pepper, and orange zest in a small bowl; mix well. Set aside.

To prepare the potatoes, combine the potatoes, 1 tablespoon oil, garlic, ½ teaspoon salt, ¼ teaspoon black pepper, and 1 teaspoon of the rosemary rub in a large bowl. Toss potatoes until well coated; set aside.

To prepare the pork chops, evenly coat each chop with the remaining rosemary rub.

Place the potatoes in the bottom of the air fryer basket. Place the chops on top of the potatoes in a single layer.

Bake at 350 degrees for 30 minutes or until done, turning halfway through.

Shrimp & Cream Cheese Wontons

8 oz. shrimp, peeled, deveined, and roughly chopped

4 oz. cream cheese, room temperature

2 cloves garlic, minced

2 green onions, thinly sliced

1 Tbsp. freshly grated ginger

1 tsp. sesame oil

1 tsp. Sriracha (optional)

salt and pepper

16 (2-inch) wonton wrappers

1 large egg, beaten

In a large bowl, combine the shrimp, cream cheese, garlic, green onions, ginger, sesame oil, and Sriracha, if using. Season with salt and pepper to taste.

To assemble the wontons, place the wrappers on a work surface. Spoon 1½ teaspoons of the mixture into the center of each wrapper. Using your finger, rub the edges of the wrappers with the beaten egg.

Fold all sides over the filling to create an "X," pinching the edges to seal.

Place the prepared wontons in a single layer in an air fryer basket. Coat the wontons with nonstick spray.

Bake for 10–12 minutes at 370 degrees, or until golden brown and crisp.

Shrimp & Cream Cheese Wonton Dipping Sauce

3 Tbsp. honey

2 Tbsp. low-sodium soy sauce

1 Tbsp. Sriracha or other hot sauce

1 tsp. vinegar or rice wine vinegar

¼ tsp. sesame oil

Mix together and serve.

Shrimp & Cream Cheese Wontons, page 112

Shrimp with Roasted Garlic-Cilantro Sauce, page 41

Shrimp with Roasted Garlic-Cilantro Sauce

Sauce

1 small head garlic

olive oil, for drizzling

1 cup chopped fresh cilantro leaves

juice of 1 lime

1 Tbsp. white wine

3 Tbsp. olive oil

2 Tbsp. chili sauce (or 1 Tbsp. dry chili flakes)

1½ lb. shrimp, raw and cleaned

Trim the top of the garlic head off, but leave the garlic intact. Place on a 12 × 12 inch piece of foil. Drizzle generously with olive oil. Wrap up garlic inside of foil to seal all the edges.

Place the foil in the air fryer basket and roast the garlic at 400 degrees for about 10–15 minutes or until slightly tender and fragrant. When ready, remove from the air fryer. Let cool.

When the garlic is cool enough to handle, squeeze the roasted garlic out of its peel and chop finely.

In a small bowl, combine the roasted garlic with the remaining sauce ingredients. Whisk together and set aside.

In a separate bowl, place shrimp and 2 tablespoons of the sauce mix. Toss to coat shrimp.

Place the shrimp in a single layer on the bottom of the air fryer basket. Bake at 370 degrees for 6–10 minutes, turning halfway. Bake in batches as needed.

Remove the shrimp from the basket and add to a bowl and coat well with the remaining roasted garlic-cilantro sauce.

Southern Buttermilk-Fried Chicken

2 chicken breasts (or legs or
   thighs. Your preference)

Marinade

2 cups buttermilk

2 tsp. salt

2 tsp. black pepper

1 tsp. cayenne pepper

Seasoned Flour

2 cups flour

1 Tbsp. baking powder

1 Tbsp. garlic powder

1 Tbsp. paprika powder

1 tsp. salt

1 tsp. pepper

Rinse the chicken and pat dry with paper towels.

For the Marinade

Toss together the chicken pieces, black pepper, cayenne pepper, and salt in a large bowl to coat. Pour the buttermilk over the chicken until it is coated. Refrigerate for at least 6 hours or overnight.

For the Seasoned Flour

In separate bowl, combine the flour, baking powder, garlic powder, paprika, salt, and pepper. Remove the chicken 1 piece at a time from the buttermilk, and dredge in the seasoned flour. Shake off any excess flour and transfer to a plate.

Arrange the chicken in 1 layer in the fryer basket with the skin-side up, spray with canola oil, and slide the basket into the air fryer.

Bake at 370 degrees for 20 minutes. Pull out the tray, turn the chicken pieces over, spray the other side, and bake for another 10 minutes.

Southern Buttermilk-Fried Chicken, page 116

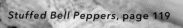
Stuffed Bell Peppers, page 119

Stuffed Bell Peppers

½ cup rice

1¾ cups water, divided

¼ cup olive oil

1 large onion, peeled and finely chopped

6 oz. ground beef

1 clove garlic, finely chopped

2 cups crushed tomatoes, divided

1 tsp. thyme

1 tsp. oregano

4 red or green bell peppers

¼ cup white wine

In a 2-cup measuring cup, combine the rice and 1½ cups water and cover tightly with plastic wrap. Cook in a microwave at 100 percent power for 4 minutes.

In a fry pan, add the beef, olive oil, and onion. Cook uncovered for about 5 minutes. Drain off excess fat.

Add 1½ cups tomatoes, garlic, thyme, oregano, and drained rice and stir to combine.

Slice off the tops of the green or red bell peppers and remove seeds. Divide stuffing among the peppers and replace tops of peppers. Place the peppers in a baking dish.

Combine ½ cup crushed tomatoes, ¼ cup white wine, and ¼ cup water and pour into bottom of dish.

Cover tightly with foil and cook for 20 minutes at 370 degrees. Poke through the foil with a knife after 10 minutes of cooking to let steam escape. Let stuffed peppers stand for about 5 minutes after cooking.

Rosemary Honey Chicken

2 chicken breasts
1 tsp. olive oil
ground pepper, to taste
sea salt, to taste

1 spring rosemary, roughly chopped
½ tsp. red pepper flakes
2 tsp. honey

Rinse the chicken breasts and pat them dry. Lightly coat the chicken all over with olive oil.

Sprinkle the skin-side up with some ground pepper, a pinch of sea salt, the dried red pepper flakes, the chopped rosemary and a drizzle of honey.

Place in the center of the air fryer basket and bake 12–15 minutes or until done at 330 degrees.

Rosemary Honey Chicken, page 120

Teriyaki Chicken Wings, page 123

Teriyaki Chicken Wings

24 chicken wings

5 Tbsp. chopped cilantro, chopped

Sauce

1 cup soy sauce

1 cup grapefruit juice

¼ cup hoisin sauce

2 Tbsp. ketchup

3 Tbsp. rice wine vinegar

¼ cup brown sugar

5 garlic cloves, minced

2 Tbsp. fresh and grated ginger

Place a 6-quart saucepan, with a steamer basket and 1 inch water in the bottom, over high heat. Cover and bring to a boil.

Place the wings into the steamer basket, cover, and reduce the heat to medium and steam for 10 minutes. Remove the wings from the basket and carefully pat dry. Lay the wings out on a cooling rack set in a half sheet pan lined with paper towels and place in the refrigerator for 1 hour.

Place the wings in an air fryer basket and bake at 330 degrees for 30 minutes, turning halfway through.

Meanwhile, combine the teriyaki sauce ingredients in a large saucepan. Simmer over low heat and reduce until slightly thickened. Pour the sauce into a large bowl.

Dump the wings into the bowl and toss to coat them with the sauce. Transfer to a serving platter and sprinkle with the cilantro.

Bang Bang Shrimp

Coating

½ cup whole milk

1 egg, beaten lightly

2 Tbsp. cornstarch

1 tsp. salt

½ tsp. garlic powder

½ tsp. cayenne pepper

½ tsp. sugar

½ tsp. paprika

½ tsp. Sriracha

Breading

1 cup panko breadcrumbs

1 lb. shrimp, peeled and deveined

Dipping Sauce

2 Tbsp. Sriracha

2 Tbsp. ketchup

¼ cup mayonnaise

Mix all the coating ingredients together in a shallow baking dish.

In a separate dish, place the panko breadcrumbs.

Dip each shrimp in the coating batter and then in the breadcrumbs. Do this one at a time and place them into the air fryer basket in a single layer. Spritz with oil.

Bake at 400 degrees for 10 minutes, turning halfway through.

Repeat with remaining shrimp.

While the shrimp are cooking, mix all dipping sauce ingredients together.

Desserts

Three-Ingredient Brownies, page 127

Three-Ingredient Brownies

¾ cup Nutella

1 egg

¼ cup flour

Mix all ingredients together. Using a nonstick spray, lightly spray a 6-inch metal round or square pan to fit in your air fryer.

Spread mixture around the pan with a spatula and bake for 10–12 minutes at 330 degrees.

Crispy Nutella Ravioli

16 wonton wrappers

1 egg, lightly beaten

1 cup Nutella

½ cup sugar

Place 1 wonton wrapper on a work surface. Brush the edges of the wrapper lightly with the beaten egg. Spoon 1 tablespoon of Nutella into the center of the wrapper. Fold the wrapper diagonally in half over the filling and press the edges of the wrapper to seal.

Repeat with the remaining wonton wrappers, egg, and Nutella.

Place the sugar on a plate.

Spray each side of the prepared wontons with a nonstick vegetable oil spray and dip each side into the sugar.

Working in batches, place a single layer in the air fryer basket and spray with nonstick spray.

Bake at 370 degrees for 8 minutes, turning over halfway through.

Cherry Hand Pies

½ cup powdered sugar
¼ tsp. ground cinnamon
pinch of nutmeg

1 can large flaky-style biscuit dough
1 (12-oz.) can cherry pie filling

In a shallow dish, mix the sugar, ground cinnamon, and nutmeg.

Roll out each section of the biscuit dough into an 8-inch round circle with a rolling pin or bottle.

Put a large spoonful of pie filling into the center of the dough. Fold over 1 side and pinch tight.

Roll the filled dough in the sugar mixture. Spray each side lightly with canola oil and place in the air fryer basket so they are not touching.

In batches, bake at 330 degrees for 10–13 minutes until golden.

Cherry Hand Pies, page 128

All Season Fruit Cobbler, page 131

All Season Fruit Cobbler

½ cup flour

¼ cup sugar

¼ cup brown sugar

⅛ tsp. butter, cold and cut into
  cubes

1 lb. plums, peaches, or
  nectarines (or a combination),
  pitted and cut lengthwise into
  ½-inch wedges

Pulse all ingredients except the fruit in a food processor until mixture begins to clump.

Spread the fruit in a baking dish and sprinkle the topping over it. You can do one large baking dish or individual ones.

Bake at 330 degrees for 17–22 minutes until golden. It will depend on the size of the fruit used.

Spanish Fried Bananas

½ cup flour

¼ tsp. salt

2 eggs, whisked

¾ cup breadcrumbs

cinnamon sugar, optional

2 large bananas

Place the flour and salt in one bowl, the eggs in another, and the breadcrumbs in a third. The cinnamon sugar should go in another bowl if you choose to use it.

Peel the bananas and cut each one into thirds. Roll the bananas in the flour, then in the egg, and finally in the breadcrumbs. Drizzle a little olive oil in a shallow dish and quickly roll the bananas in it.

Place 4–5 pieces directly into the air fryer basket and bake at 350 degrees for 8 minutes. At 4 minutes, take the basket out and give it a little shake to move the bananas. Continue frying, and then remove the finished bananas and drop them directly into the cinnamon sugar or onto a serving plate. Allow to cool for 1 minute.

Note: Make your own cinnamon sugar by combining ½ cup sugar and ¼ teaspoon cinnamon.

Chocolate Molten Lava Cakes

⅓ cup butter, plus more for greasing the ramekins

cocoa powder, for dusting

½ cup chocolate chips or chopped chocolate

¼ cup sugar

2 Tbsp. flour

2 eggs

Grease the inside of 4 (8-oz.) ramekins with the butter, dust with the cocoa powder, and tap out any extra.

Place the chocolate chips and butter in a medium microwave-safe bowl and microwave in 30-second increments, stirring between each increment until the chocolate is melted and smooth.

Stir the sugar and flour into the chocolate mixture. Add in the eggs and mix until smooth.

Pour the batter into the 4 ramekins; they should be about ½ full. Place the ramekins in an air fryer basket.

Bake at 330 degrees for 12–15 minutes, until the top and edges are set, but the center is still jiggly. Let cool slightly for 2–3 minutes. Be careful, because ramekins may still be hot. Serve immediately.

Chocolate Molten Lava Cakes, page 132

Jam Baked Apples, page 135

Jam Baked Apples

2 apples (I recommend Fuji or McIntosh)

1 tsp. lemon juice

¼ cup strawberry jam, jelly, or preserves

2 Tbsp. flour

3 Tbsp. butter, cold and diced

3 Tbsp. brown sugar

½ cup uncooked oats

¼ tsp. ground cinnamon

pinch of salt

Cut each apple in half along its equator. Using a melon baller, cut out each side of the core, creating a rounded hole. Rub the inside of the open apple with lemon juice. Place 1 tablespoon of jam into each hole.

To make the topping, mix together the flour, butter, brown sugar, oats, cinnamon, and salt in a small bowl. Press this mixture on the top of each apple half, covering the jam.

Place the prepared apples in a baking dish filled with about ¼-inch water. Bake at 330 degrees until the tops are golden brown and the apples are tender, 20–30 minutes.

Nutella Flake Pastry

1 can refrigerated crescent dinner rolls

8 Tbsp. Nutella

1 egg, lightly beaten

Open the crescent roll can. Keep the large squares intact. You should have 4 per can. Pinch all the seams together.

Place 2 tablespoons of the Nutella in the center of each square and fold the dough over to make a triangle. Brush lightly with the beaten egg.

Bake in batches at 350 degrees for 10-12 minutes until golden.

Nutella Flake Pastry, page 136

Lemon Sponge Cake, page 139

Lemon Sponge Cake

Cake

1 cup flour

1 cup sugar

8 oz. butter, room temperature

3 eggs

1 tsp. baking powder

1 Tbsp. lemon zest

Glaze

¼ cup powdered sugar, plus more
  for topping

2 Tbsp. milk

2 Tbsp. lemon juice

Spray 2 (6-inch) metal baking pans with nonstick spray.

Place all the cake ingredients in a bowl and mix with a hand mixer until thick and creamy.

Place half of the batter in each pan. Bake at 350 degrees for 15 minutes until golden.

While baking, prepare glaze by mixing all the ingredients together. When the cakes are done, remove them from the air fryer and drizzle each cake with ½ of the glaze. Sprinkle with powdered sugar.

Pecan Pie Bread Pudding

6 slices bread, white or French, day-old or toasted.

2 eggs, lightly beaten

1¼ cups milk

½ cup half-and-half

½ cup sugar

¼ tsp. salt

½ Tbsp. vanilla extract

4 Tbsp. butter, softened

¾ cup brown sugar

½ cup chopped pecans

Cut the bread into cubes and place in a large bowl.

In another bowl, beat the eggs, milk, half-and-half, sugar, salt, and vanilla. Pour over bread. Allow this mixture to sit 5–10 minutes

In another small bowl, combine the softened butter, brown sugar, and pecans with a fork. The mixture will have the consistency of wet sand.

Pour half of the bread mixture into 2 mini loaf pans.

Top with half the pecan mixture.

Spoon the remaining bread mixture over the 2 loaves and top with the remaining pecan mixture. Press the mix down into each pan slightly. The pans will be really full.

Place in the air fryer basket and bake at 310 degrees for approximately 30 minutes. Bake in batches if needed. The center will a little jiggly but will set when it is cooled.

Pecan Pie Bread Pudding, page 140

Sweet Dark Cherry Clafoutis, page 143

Sweet Dark Cherry Clafoutis

2 cups pitted sweet cherries
1 cup whole milk
¼ cup heavy cream
½ cup cake flour
4 eggs

½ cup sugar
⅛ tsp. salt
½ tsp. pure almond extract
powdered sugar, for dusting

Butter 2 mini 5-inch pie pans. Arrange the cherries in the pans.

In a saucepan over medium-low heat, heat the milk and cream until small bubbles appear around the edges of the pan.

Remove the pan from the heat and vigorously whisk in the flour, a little at a time, until no lumps remain.

In a bowl, whisk together the eggs, sugar, and salt until creamy. Whisk in the milk mixture and the almond extract. Pour this over the cherries.

Place 1 pie pan on a baking sheet. Bake at 330 degrees for 15–20 minutes, until browned. Transfer to a rack to cool. Dust with powdered sugar and serve warm.

Chocolate Chip Mini Cheesecakes

Crust

1 cup graham cracker crumbs

2 Tbsp. brown sugar

¼ tsp. salt

2½ Tbsp. butter, melted

Cheesecake

1 (8-oz.) pkg. cream cheese, softened

2 Tbsp. sour cream

⅓ cup sugar

1 egg

1 tsp. vanilla extract

1 cup chocolate chips

Line 8 cups of a mini muffin pan with paper liners.

For the Crust:

In a medium bowl, mix together the graham cracker crumbs, brown sugar, and salt. Pour melted butter over the mix and stir with a fork to moisten the crumb mixture.

Place about a tablespoon of the crumb mixture in each of the prepared muffin cups and pack down into an even layer.

For the Cheesecake:

In a large bowl, cream together the cream cheese, sour cream, and sugar until smooth. Beat in the egg and vanilla extract.

Place 1 tablespoon chocolate chips into each of the muffin cups. Evenly divide cheesecake batter between the muffin cups, covering the first layer of chocolate chips. Place another tablespoon of chocolate chips on top of the cheesecake batter in each of the muffin cups.

Bake for 18–23 minutes at 330 degrees, until cheesecakes are set. Bake in batches as needed.

Allow the cheesecakes to cool for 10 minutes in the muffin pan. Then carefully transfer the cheesecakes to a cooling rack to cool completely and store in the refrigerator.

Chocolate Chip Mini Cheesecakes, page 144

Wild Berry Cheesecake Roll, page 147

Wild Berry Cheesecake Roll

1 (8-oz.) pkg. cream cheese
½ cup powdered sugar
1 tsp. vanilla extract
16 egg roll wrappers

2 cups chopped strawberries
2 cups blueberries
cinnamon sugar, for topping

Spray a baking sheet with nonstick cooking spray and set aside.

Combine the cream cheese, powdered sugar, and vanilla in a bowl and whip together.

Scoop about 1 tablespoon of the mixture onto an egg roll wrap that's been laid out on a clean dry surface. Next, add a small scoop of strawberries and blueberries.

Working the egg roll wrapper in a diamond configuration, roll the bottom corner up over the ingredients tightly. Next, fold the left and right sides over. Then finish rolling the wrapper. Use a little bit of water to seal the flap down.

Place a cheesecake roll on a baking sheet sprayed with nonstick spray. Spray each roll with nonstick spray and sprinkle with cinnamon sugar.

Bake in batches at 375 degrees for about 10 minutes or until golden brown. Turn over halfway through.

Apple Pie Roll-Ups

16 egg roll wrappers

1 (12-oz.) can apple pie filling

½ cup powdered sugar

1 Tbsp. cinnamon

⅛ tsp. nutmeg

4 Tbsp. butter, melted

Place the wraps on a clean, dry surface. Have each wrap facing out on the diagonal so that it is a diamond shape.

Place 2 tablespoons of the pie filling in the center of a wrapper. With your finger, seal the outside of all edges with water and fold up the wrapper like a burrito. Repeat with remaining wrappers.

Lightly spray with canola oil and place in a single layer, not touching, in the air fryer basket. Bake in batches at 350 degrees for 8–10 minutes until golden.

While baking, combine the powdered sugar, cinnamon, and nutmeg.

Remove the roll-ups from the basket and brush with melted butter. Sift the powdered sugar mixture on top while warm.

Easy Cannoli Cups

Wonton Cups

24 wonton wrappers

Filling

3 cups ricotta cheese

1⅓ cups powdered sugar

1 tsp. vanilla extract

⅓ cup semi-sweet mini chocolate chips

For the Wonton Cups

Place each wonton wrapper in the base of a mini cupcake pan, pressing down to create a mini bowl.

Bake at 350 degrees for 5 minutes until the cups are lightly browned.

Allow to cool fully before filling with the ricotta mixture.

For the Filling

Place the ricotta and vanilla in a medium-sized mixing bowl. Mix until smooth, about 2 minutes. Slowly add in the powdered sugar, mixing until just combined.

Stir in the chocolate chips. Fill the wonton cups ¾ full with filling and top with extra chips!

Index

About the Author

Growing up in the chocolate industry inspired a journey filled with delicious and innovative cuisine for **Allison Waggoner**. Allison began her career developing her family's gourmet chocolates, creating some of the finest award-winning confections in the world. Her culinary designs have been featured in Crate & Barrel, *Culinary Product Magazine*, Ghirardelli Chocolate Company, Godiva Chocolatier, Walt Disney World, *Fancy Food Magazine*, Target, Universal Studios, Williams-Sonoma, and on The Food Network.

As a classically trained chef, Allison's culinary and marketing career brought her to the attention of television executives. She first appeared as a guest host, bringing her confections and family history to the home shopping industry. Allison is presently seen in more than eighty million homes as a host on *EVINE Live*, a leader in retail broadcasting. She enjoys working "in the kitchen" with her friends Paula Deen, Todd English, and Kevin Dundon.

Now, Allison brings her love of food and favorite recipes to you in her third cookbook. Her first book, *In the Kitchen: A Collection of Home and Family Memories*, was released in 2014. Her second is a nostalgic collection of recipes to celebrate the moments in our lives. *In the Kitchen: A Gathering of Friends* is filled with simple, delicious dishes for every day of the week.

Allison lives in the Twin Cities, Minnesota.

Visit her at www.allisonwaggoner.com.